NEIL A. KJOS
PIANO LIBRARY

LEVEL FOUR

ESSENTIAL PIANO REPERTOIRE

From the 17th, 18th, & 19th Centuries

SELECTED & EDITED BY

Keith Snell

ISBN 0-8497-6354-1

THE NEIL A. KJOS PIANO LIBRARY

The **Neil A. Kjos Piano Library** is a comprehensive series of piano music in a wide variety of musical styles. The library is divided into eleven levels and will provide students with a complete performance experience in both solo and ensemble music. Teachers will find the carefully graded levels appropriate when choosing repertoire for evaluations, auditions, festivals, and examinations. Included in the **Neil A. Kjos Piano Library:**

Preparatory Level – Level Ten

Fundamentals of Piano Theory
Piano Repertoire: Baroque & Classical
Piano Repertoire: Romantic & 20th Century
Piano Repertoire: Etudes
Scale Skills
Essential Piano Repertoire
Music of the 21st Century
New Age Piano
Jazz Piano
One Piano Four Hands
Music for Christmas

PREFACE

Essential Piano Repertoire from the ***Neil A. Kjos Piano Library*** provides piano students with carefully chosen collections of the very best keyboard literature from the 17th, 18th, and 19th Centuries. The appropriately graded levels ensure steady and thorough progress as pianists advance in their study of the baroque, classical, and romantic styles.

Compact disc recordings, performed by pianist Diane Hidy, are included in each volume of ***Essential Piano Repertoire***. The interpretations follow the editions closely as practical examples for students.

CONTENTS

Sonata

L. 423

Track 1

Domenico Scarlatti
(1685-1757)

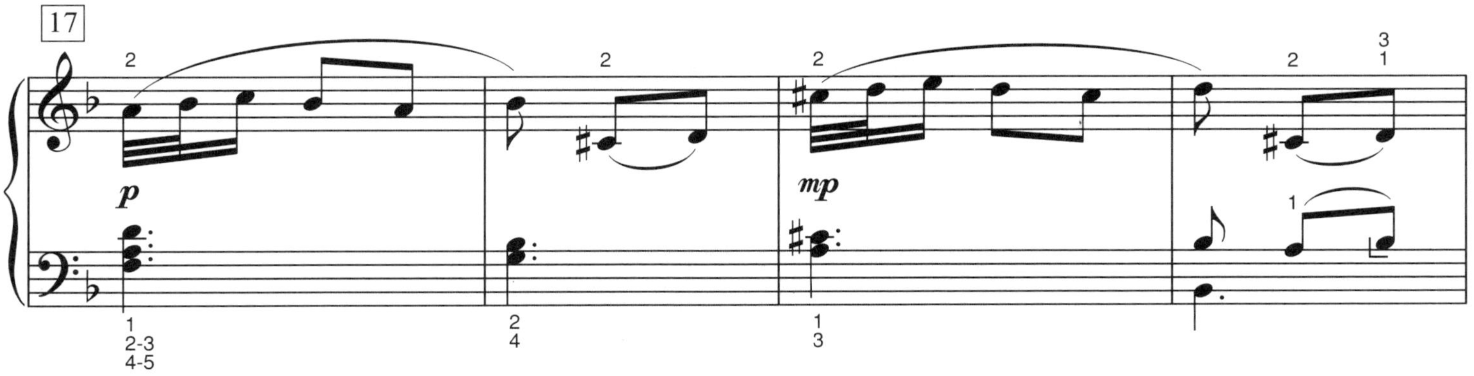

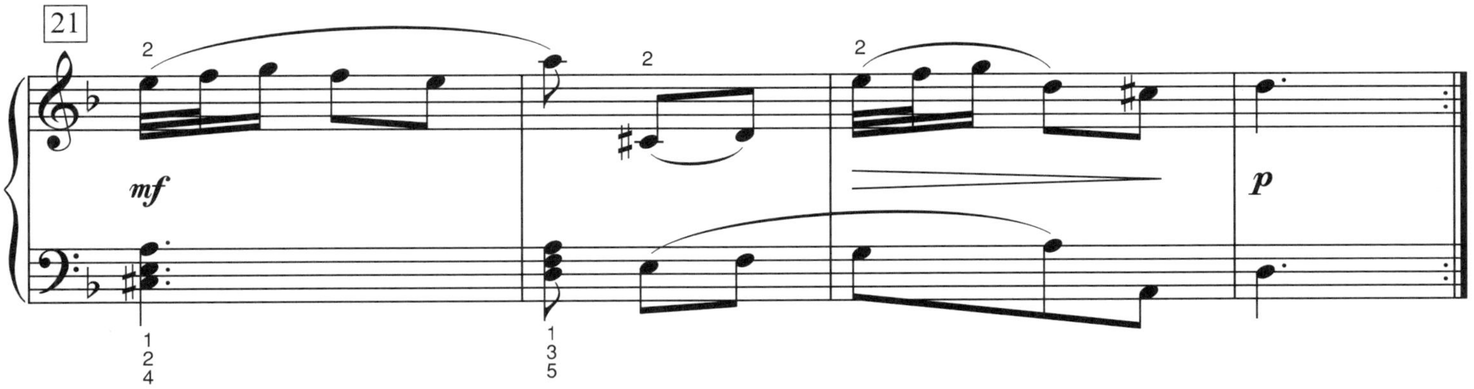

Minuet

From the Notebook for Anna Magdalena Bach (1725)

Track 2

Johann Sebastian Bach
(1685-1750)

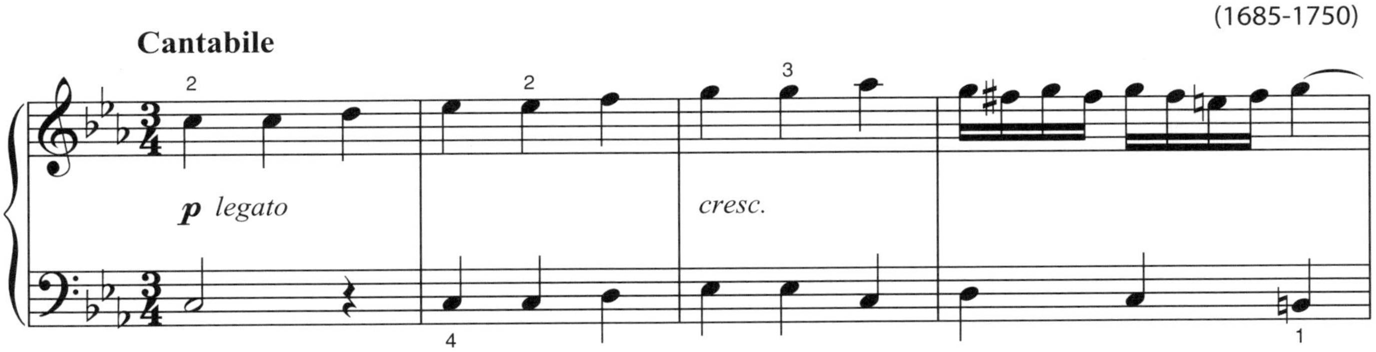

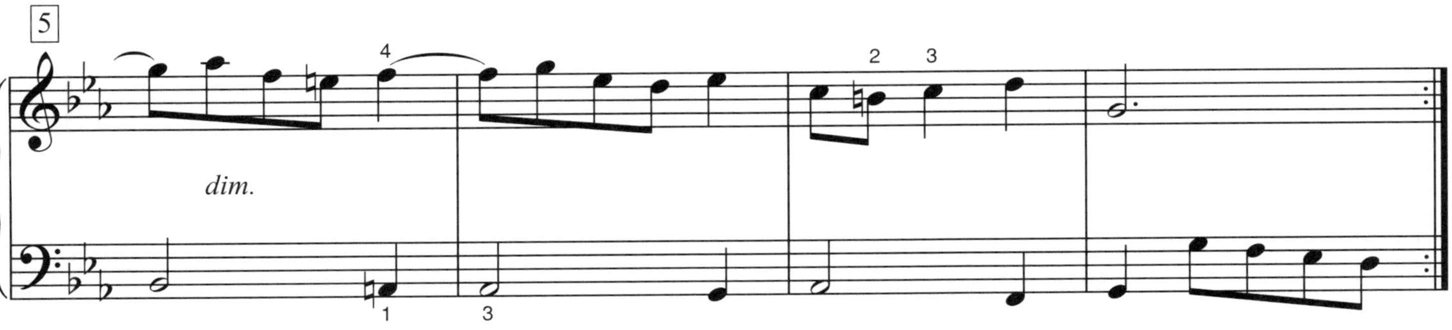

9
mf
13
mp
17
p
cresc.
21
f
p

Prelude

BWV 939

From *Eighteen Little Preludes*

Track 3

Johann Sebastian Bach
(1685-1750)

Polonaise

BWV Anh. 125

From the *Notebook for Anna Magdalena Bach*

Track 4

Carl Philipp Emanuel Bach
(1714-1788)

13
p cresc.
dim.
16
19
f
22

Sonatina

Op. 36, No. 2

Track 5

I.

Muzio Clementi
(1752-1832)

23
p
fz
p
27
fz
p
cresc.
31
f
mp
mf
f
35
p
legato
39
fz

43
p
47
cresc.
f
p
legato
51
cresc.
f
55

II.

Track 6

III. Rondo

Track 7

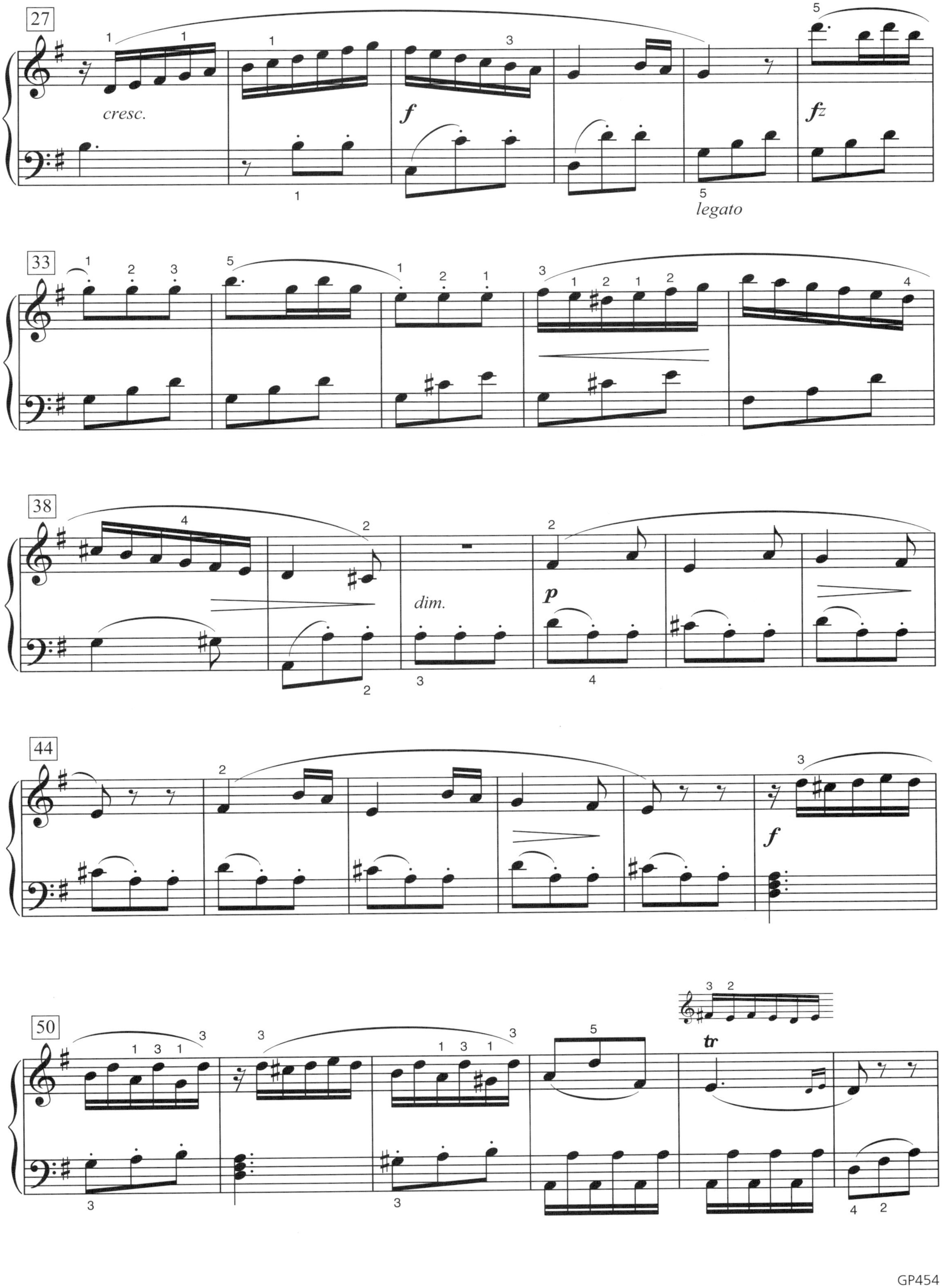
27
cresc.
legato
33
38
dim.
44
50
tr

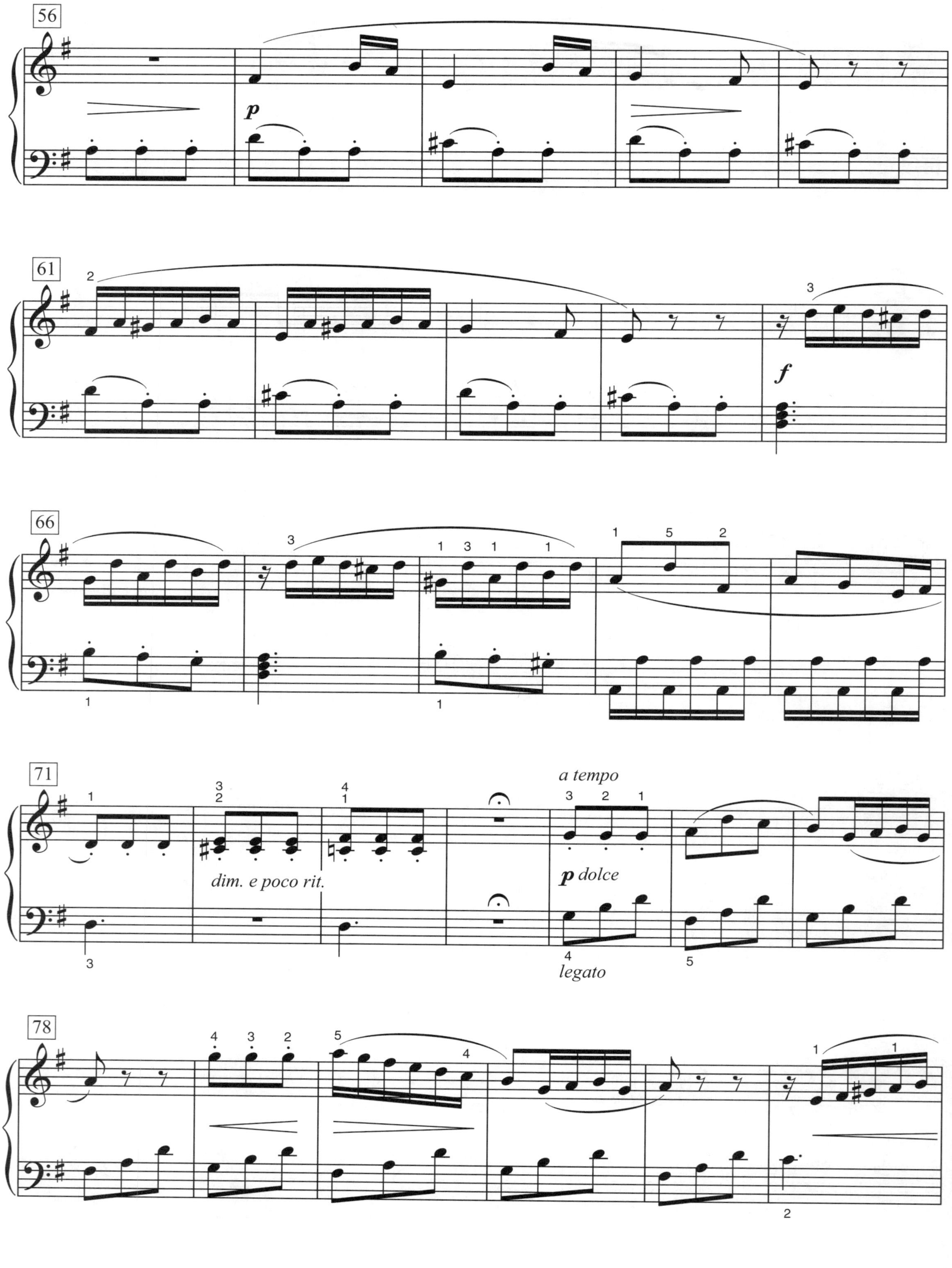
56
61
66
71
a tempo
dim. e poco rit.
p dolce
legato
78

84
89
95
101
cresc.
106

Sonatina

I.

Track 8

Ludwig van Beethoven
(1770-1827)

23
f
27
mf
mp
32
mf
37
dim.
p
43
p
mp
mf
dim.
legato

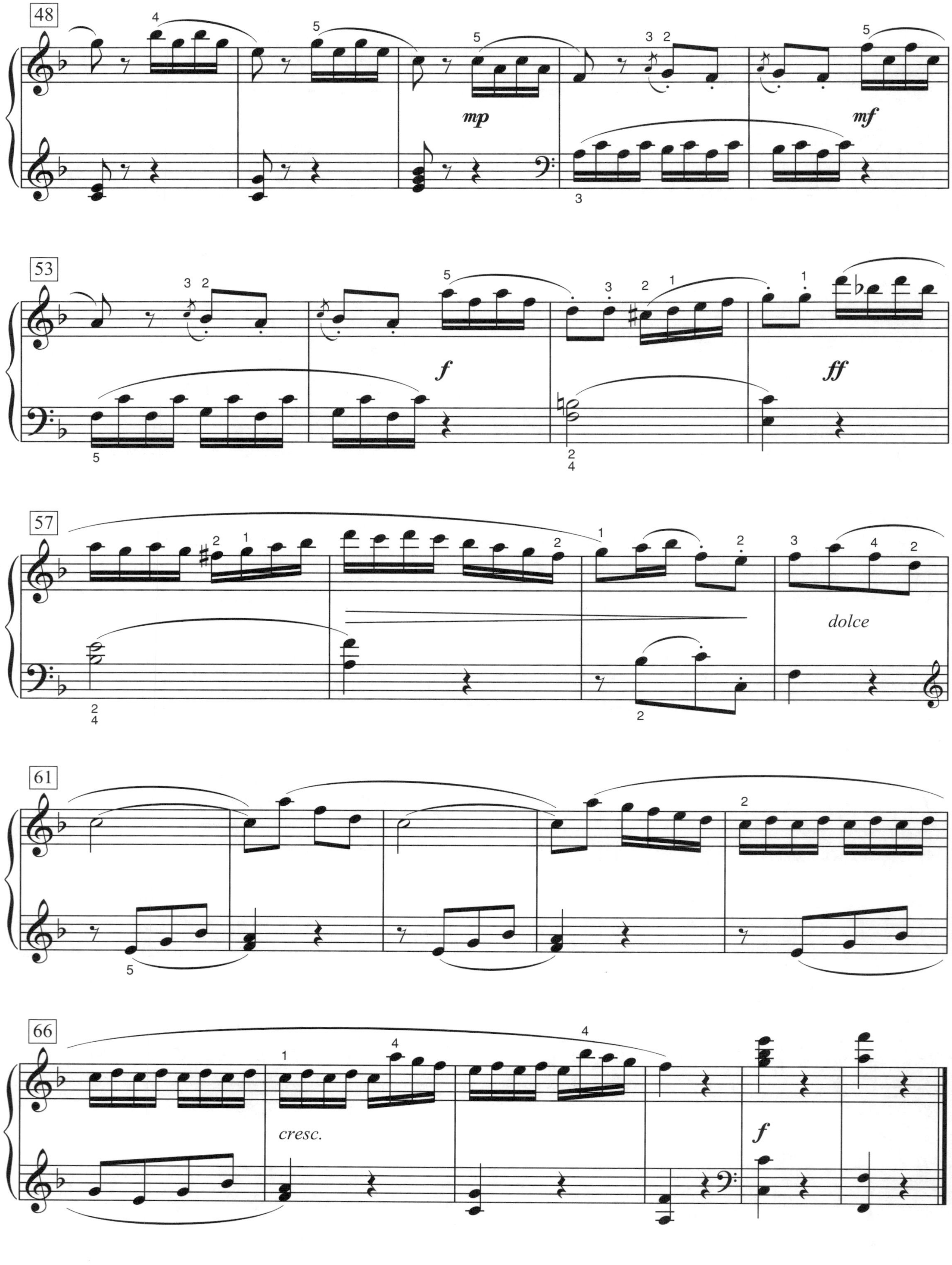
48
mp
mf
53
f
ff
57
dolce
61
66
cresc.
f

II. Rondo

Track 9

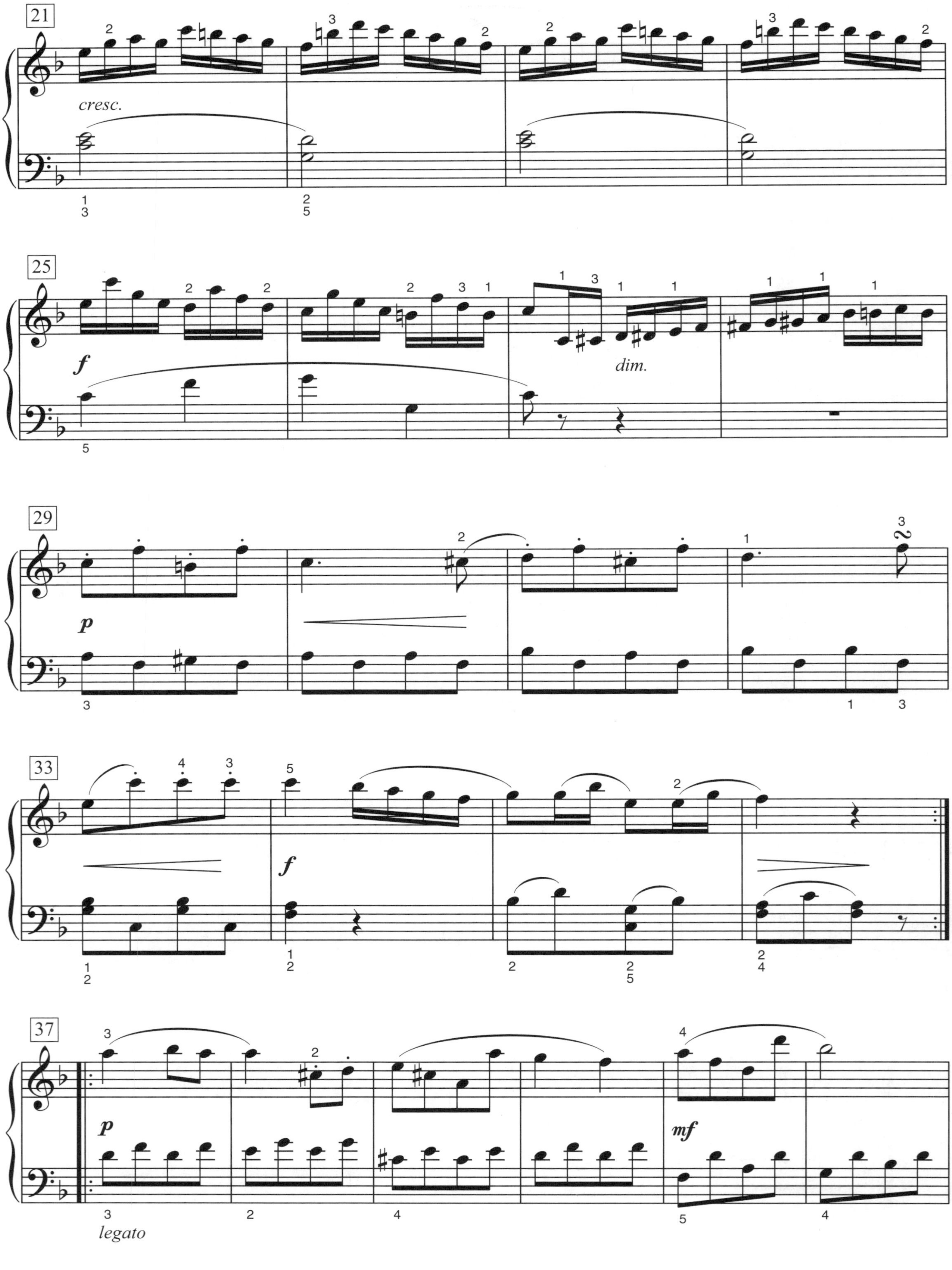
21
cresc.
25
f
dim.
29
p
33
f
37
p
mf
legato

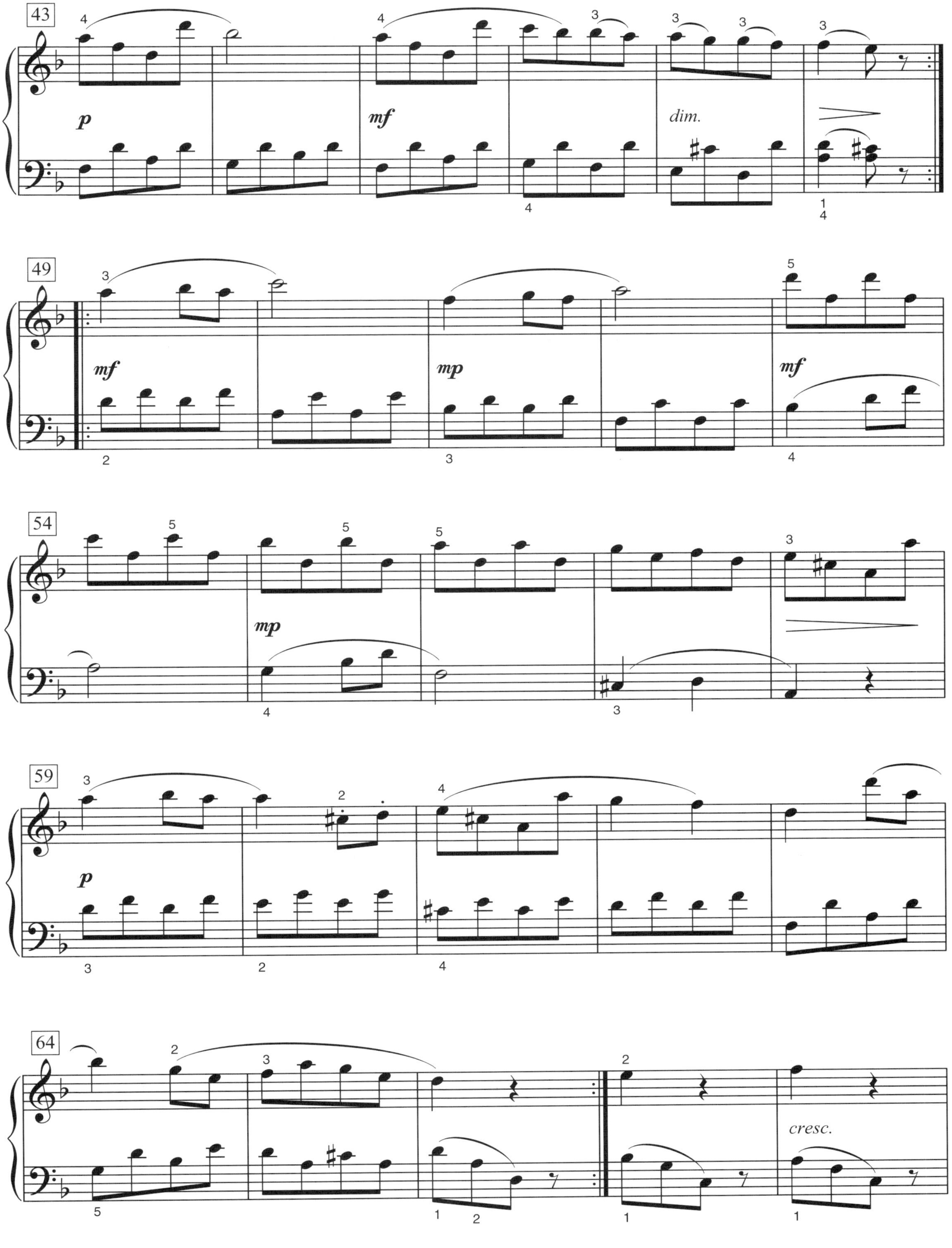
43
p
mf
dim.
49
mf
mp
mf
54
mp
59
p
64
cresc.

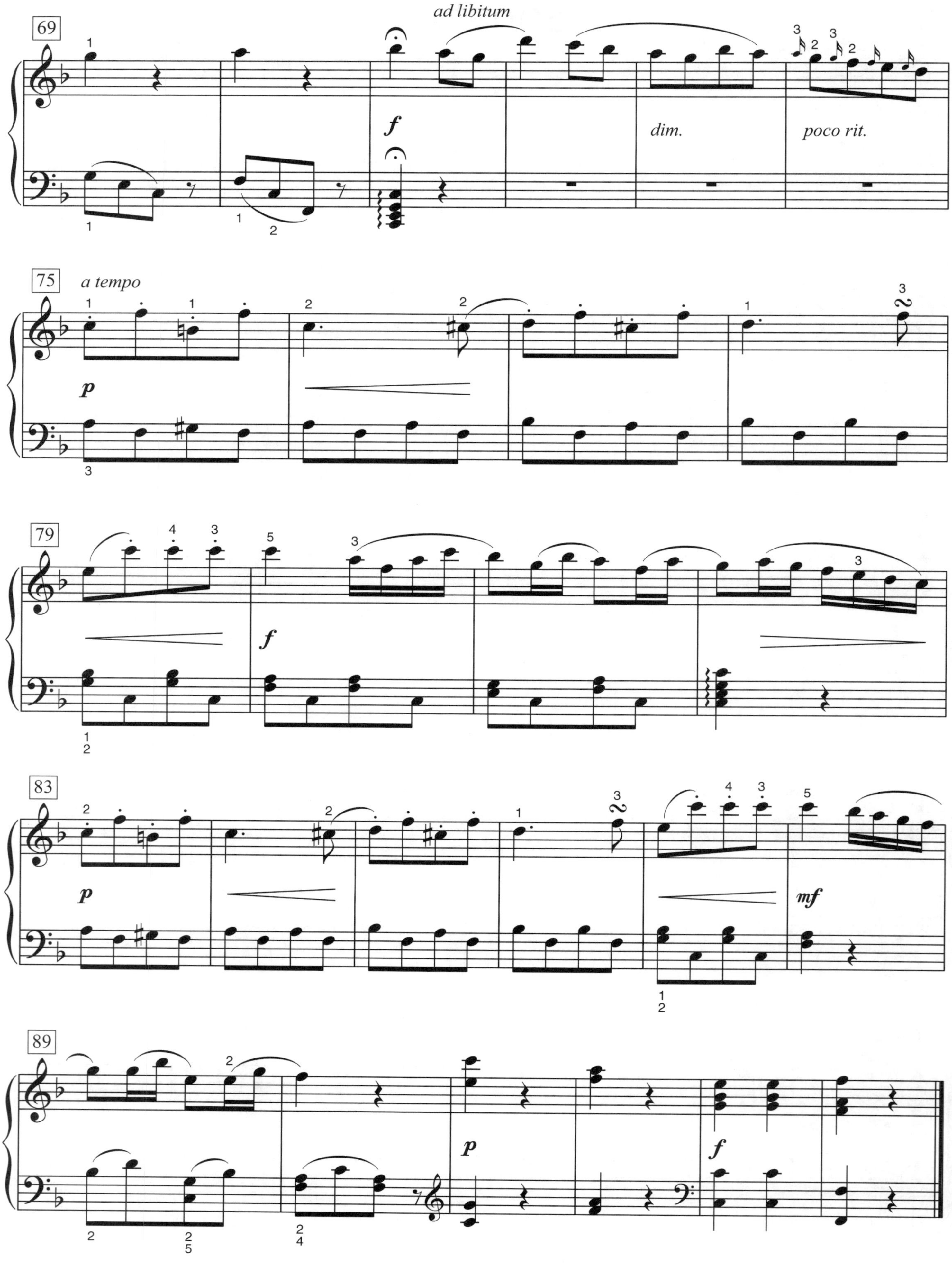
69
ad libitum
f
dim.
poco rit.
75
a tempo
p
79
f
83
p
mf
89
p
f

Sonatina

Op. 55, No. 1

I.

Track 10

Friedrich Kuhlau
(1786-1832)

Allegro

21
p dolce
f
25
mf
29
p
cresc.
33
f
p
37
mf

dim.
dolce
cresc.

II. Rondo

Track 11

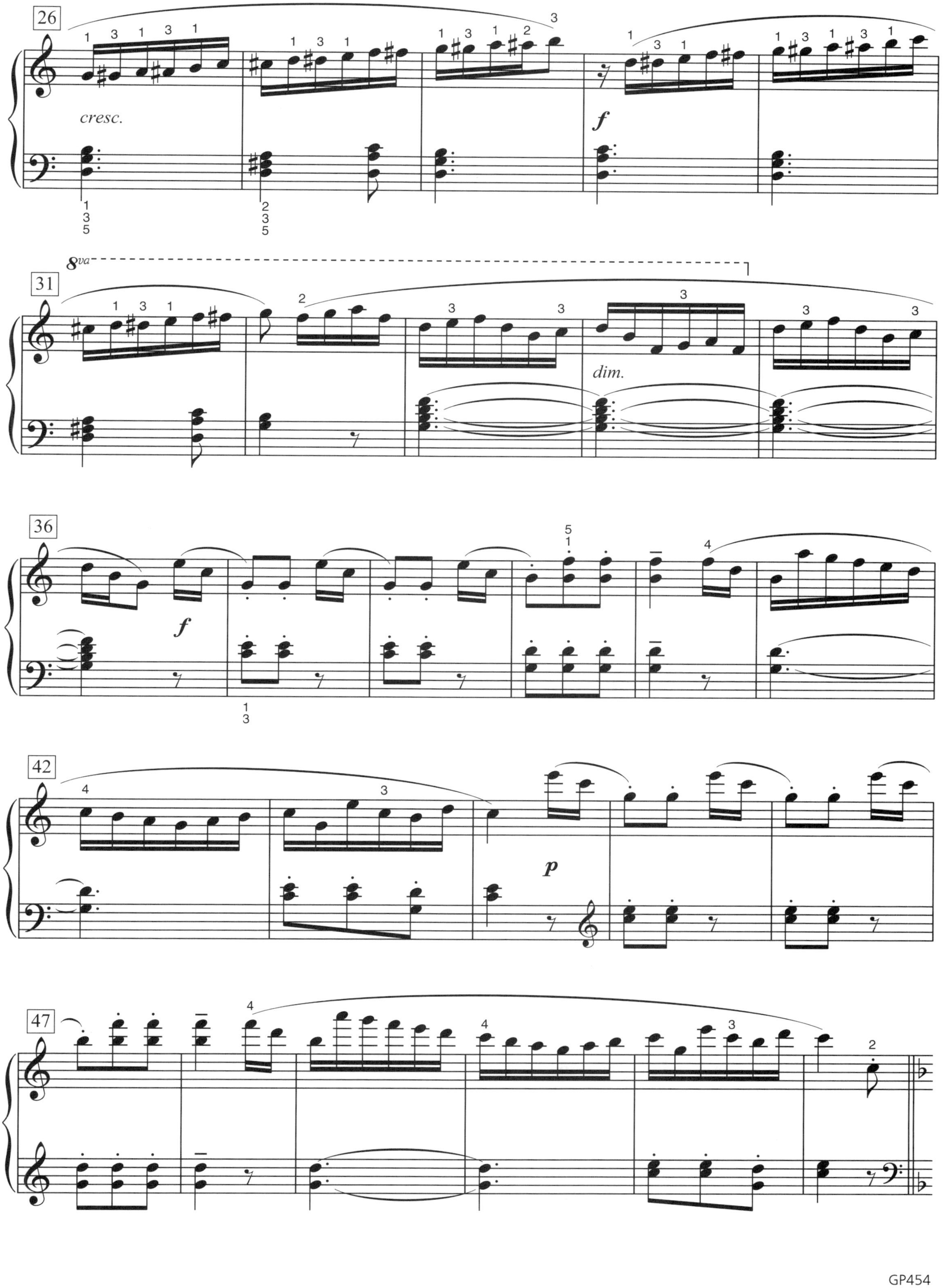
26
cresc.
f
31
8va
dim.
36
f
42
p
47

53
dolce
60
67
dim.
p
cresc.
74
p
81
p
sf

87
mf
93
f
sf
p
cresc.
8va
99
f
(8)
104
p
f
110
p
f
ff

Waltz

Op. 18, No. 5

Track 12

Franz Schubert
(1797-1828)

17
mf
p
21
mf
p
25
pp
29
mf
1.
2.

Ballade

Op. 100, No. 15

Track 13

Friedrich Burgmüller
(1806-1874)

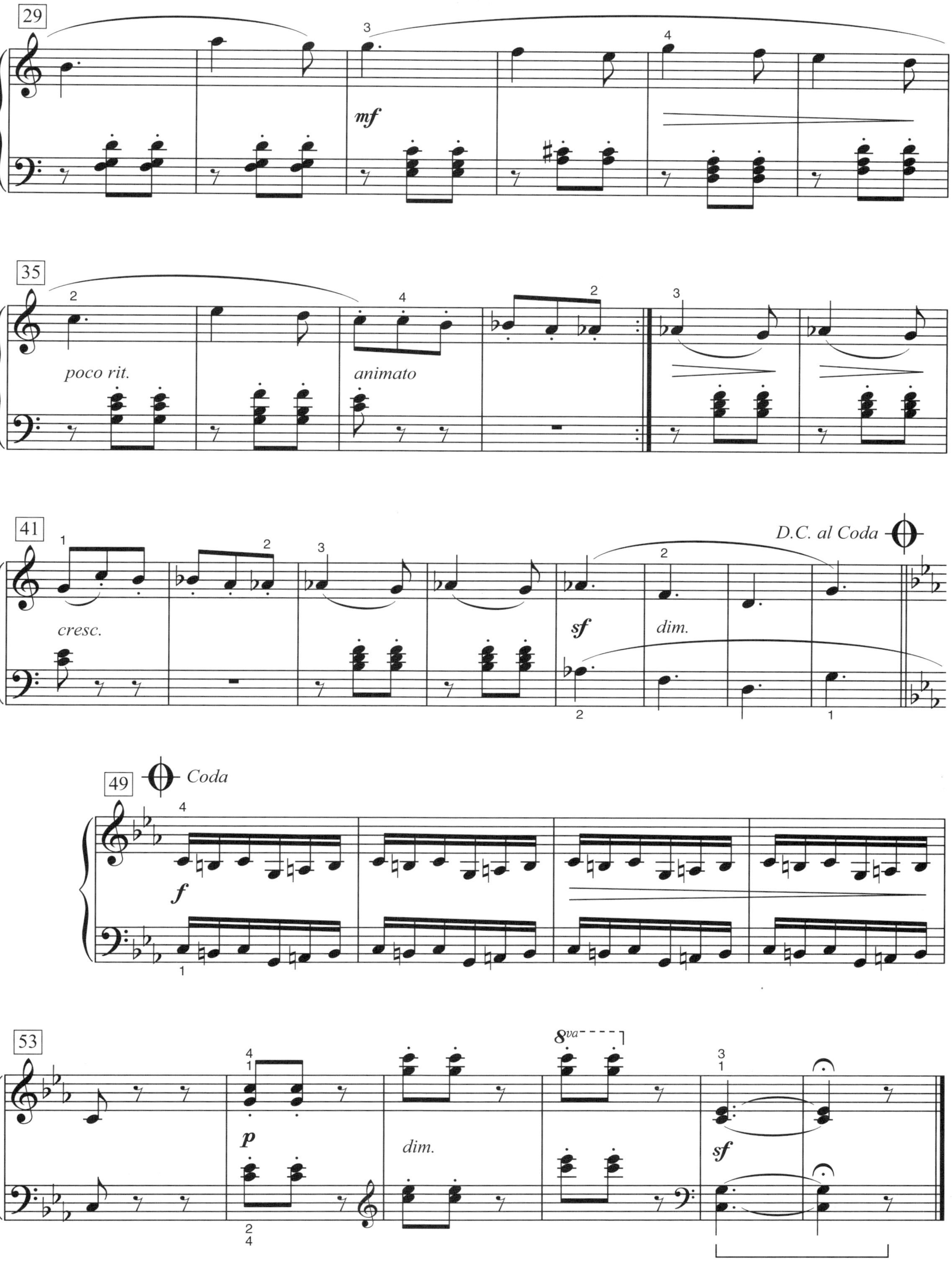
29
mf
35
poco rit.
animato
41
cresc.
sf
dim.
D.C. al Coda
49
Coda
f
53
p
dim.
8va
sf

Hunting Song

Op. 68, No. 7

Track 14

Robert Schumann
(1810-1856)

Frisch und Fröhlich
Briskly and Cheerfully

17
ff
p
ff
21
p
f
25
29
33

Sonatina

Op. 157, No. 4

I.

Track 15

Fritz Spindler
(1817-1905)

Allegro moderato

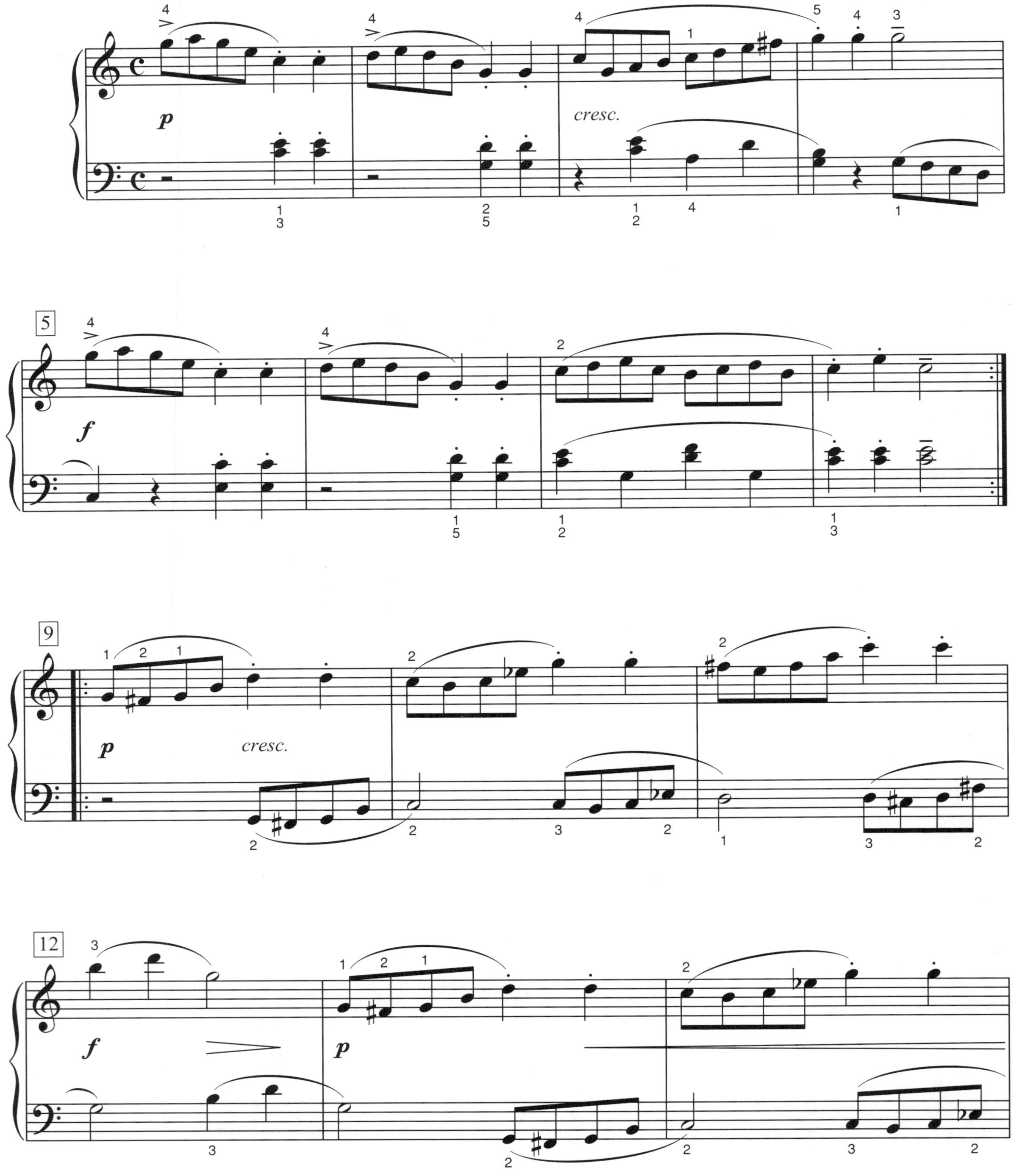

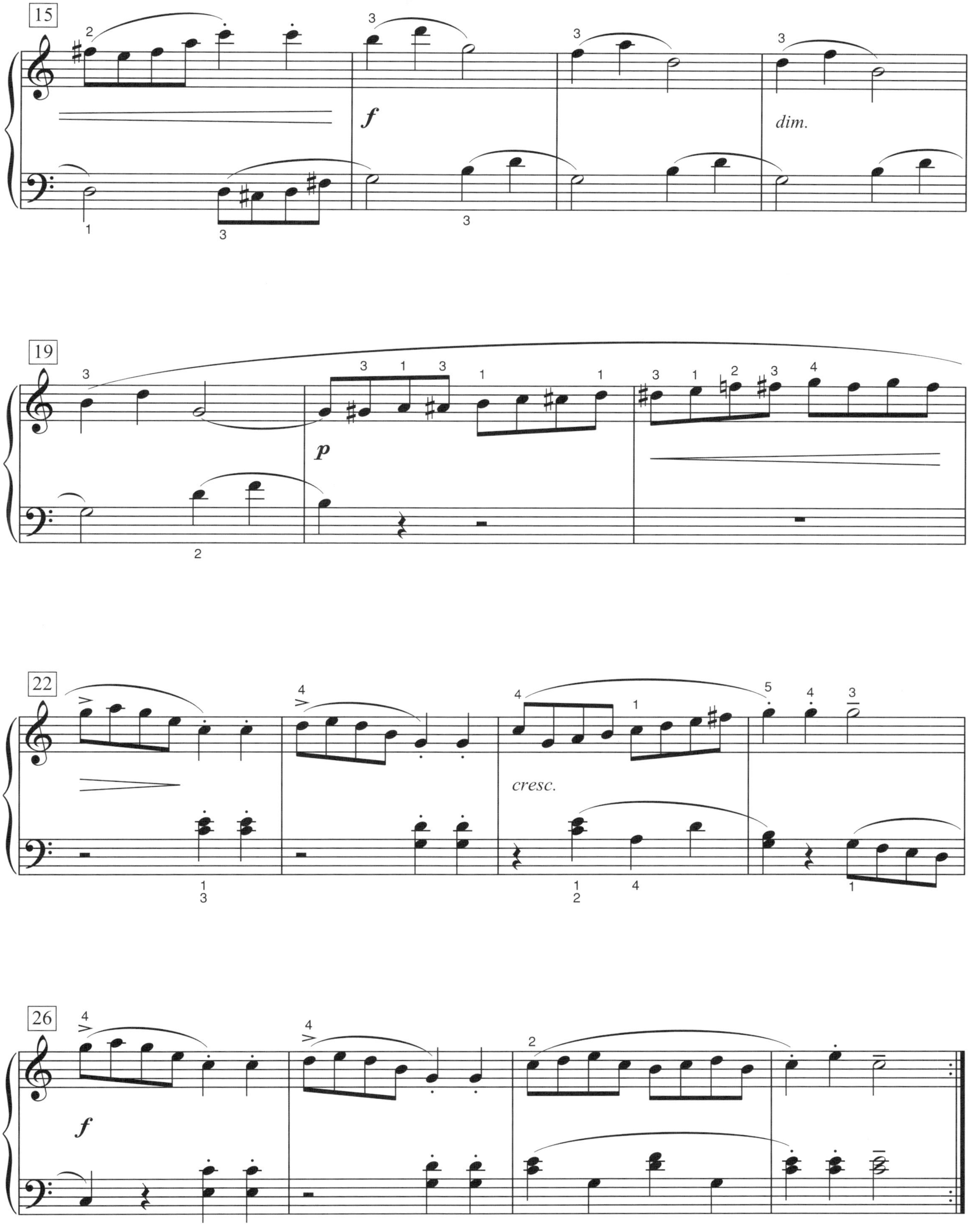
15
f
dim.
19
p
22
cresc.
26
f

II.

Track 16

17
cresc.
21
f
25
29
ff
mf
33
ff
mf
mp

37
mf
41
45
50
54
p
cresc.

58
f
62
66
p
legato
cresc.
71
f

The Sick Doll

Op. 39, No. 6

Track 17

Peter Ilyich Tchaikovsky
(1840-1893)

21
f
dim.
26
rit.
31
a tempo
mf
p
37
pp
rit.

Elfin Dance

Op. 12, No. 4

Track 18

Edvard Grieg
(1843-1907)

26
f
p
dim.
31
36
fz
pp
41
46
ppp

Novelette Romantique

Op. 176, No. 18

Track 19

Jean Baptiste Duvernoy
(1842-1907)

17
f marcato
21
25
f marcato
29
33
p

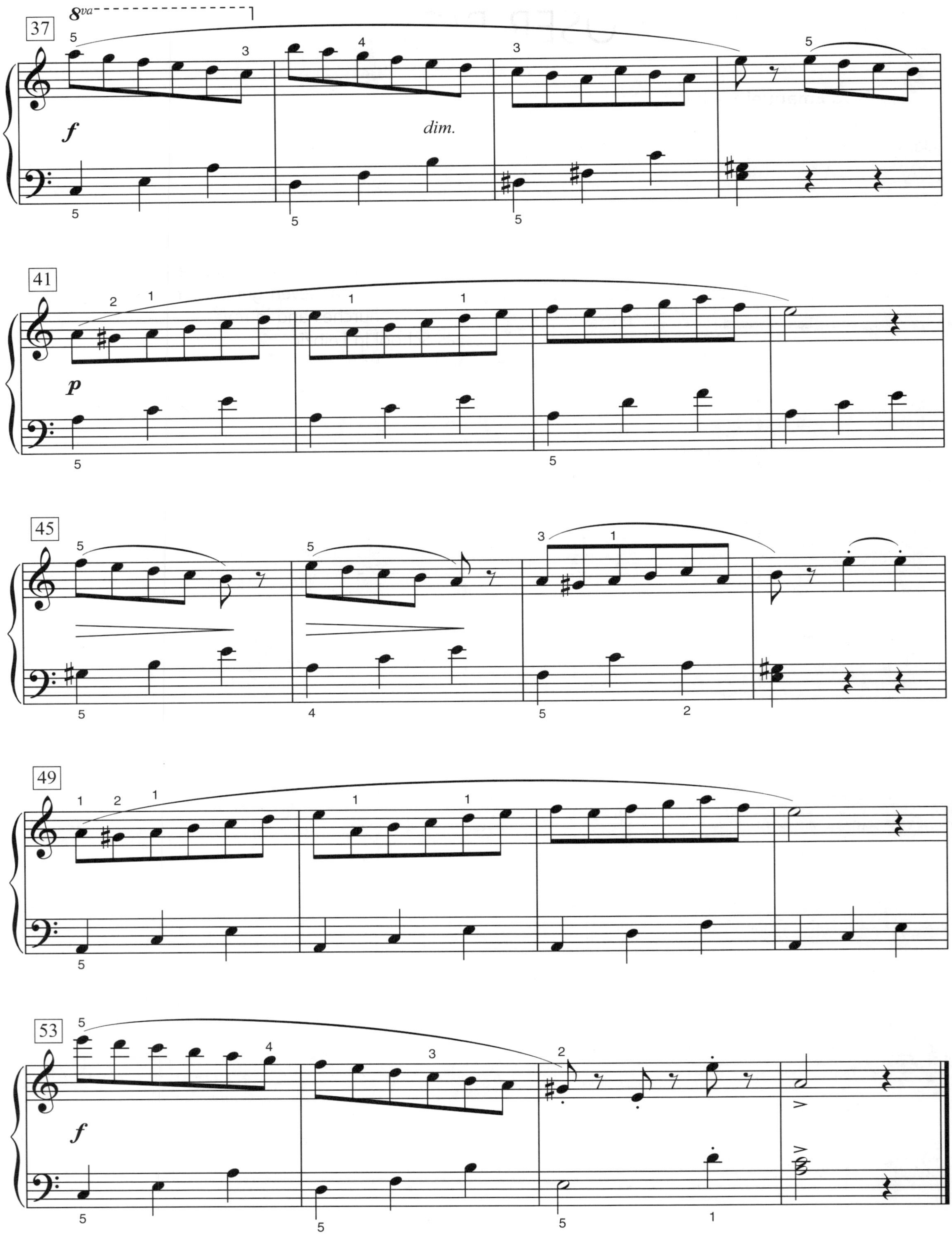
8va
37
f
dim.
41
p
45
49
53
f

COMPOSER BIOGRAPHIES

Carl Philipp Emanuel Bach (1714–1788) was a German composer and the second son of J.S. Bach. Widely acclaimed throughout Europe, he was the leading court musician of Frederick the Great in Berlin. His pre-classical style was important during the transition from the Baroque period into the Classical period. His keyboard works influenced composers such as Haydn, Mozart, and Beethoven. His essay *True Art of Keyboard Playing* is one of the first important piano methods, and a definitive source on the style and performance practices of his time.

Johann Sebastian Bach (1685–1750) was a German composer, regarded as the greatest composer of the Baroque period. He had numerous relatives who were musicians: from seven generations, 193 out of 200 were musicians. Throughout his life, he held positions at various churches and in royal courts, and for almost thirty years he was the director of music at the St. Thomas School in Leipzig. He was married twice and had twenty children, several of whom became well known musicians. Bach was a prolific composer: his complete works fill forty-six large volumes containing choral music, concertos, orchestral and chamber works, and organ and clavier (keyboard) music.

Ludwig van Beethoven (1770–1827) was a German composer and pianist. Beethoven's father insisted that Beethoven practice long hours in hopes he would become a child prodigy like Mozart. In 1787 he visited Vienna, where he played for Mozart, who predicted an outstanding musical career for Beethoven. In 1792 he studied with Haydn for a year. At this time, Beethoven began to earn his living from the sale of compositions and from teaching. He became an honored and respected musician to many royal families. In his early thirties, Beethoven experienced hearing loss which later resulted in total deafness. A prolific composer, Beethoven wrote thirty-two piano sonatas, five piano concertos, one violin concerto, nine symphonies, an opera, a great quantity of chamber music, and many other works.

Friedrich Burgmüller (1806–1874), a German composer, came from a musical family. He moved to Paris in 1832, where he enjoyed a considerable reputation as a pianist, composer, and piano teacher. Burgmüller is particularly noted for his three sets of etudes for piano: *Op. 100, Op. 105*, and *Op. 109*.

Muzio Clementi (1752–1832) was a famous Italian pianist, composer, and teacher. In 1781, he and Mozart had a contest to determine which one was the better pianist. Although no winner was announced, Clementi was thought to have a better technique, but the audience felt that Mozart was a better musician. Clementi wrote *The Art of Playing on the Piano-Forte*, a method which he used with his beginning students. Chopin also used this book with his students. In addition to his teaching, composing, and performing, Clementi established a successful piano factory and a publishing company.

Jean Baptiste Duvernoy (1842–1907) was a French pianist and composer. Duvernoy studied at the Paris Conservatory, where he later became a professor of piano. He composed many pieces for instructional purposes.

Edvard Grieg (1843–1907), born in Bergen, Norway, was a famous pianist and composer during his lifetime. His writing style is unique for its use of Norwegian folksong. His most frequently performed works are the *Lyric Pieces for Piano*, and the *Piano Concerto in A Minor*. Grieg also wrote many works for orchestra, including the suite *Peer Gynt*.

Friedrich Kuhlau (1786–1832) was born in Hamburg, Germany, where he was highly regarded as a pianist, piano teacher, and composer. In 1810, he moved to Copenhagen, Denmark. There he became known as the Great Danish Composer when he composed several successful operas which used popular national songs. In 1825, Kuhlau gained the respect and friendship of Ludwig van Beethoven during a visit to Vienna. It was on this occasion that Beethoven wrote a humorous canon on Kuhlau's name: *Kuhl, nicht lau* – cool, not lukewarm! Today, Kuhlau is best known for his sonatas and sonatinas for the piano and his many works for the flute.

Domenico Scarlatti (1685–1757) was the son of the composer Alessandro Scarlatti. Although born and raised in Naples, Italy, Domenico spent most of his career in Madrid, Spain, under the patronage of Queen Maria Barbara. He wrote more than five hundred short pieces for the harpsichord. Although he titled most of these works sonatas, they are similar to brief etudes which use one particular device or figuration. His keyboard music is colorful and original and is played frequently in concert by harpsichordists and pianists.

Franz Schubert (1797–1828), an Austrian composer, began violin lessons when he was eight. He was also given lessons on the piano and the organ, in singing, and in composition. He followed his father's occupation as a teacher in an elementary school, but taught unsuccessfully for three years. During these years, he devoted his leisure time to composing songs, and in one year alone (1815), he composed 144 songs. He struggled continually to make a living, although he was recognized as a composer of genius. He was disgracefully underpaid by his publishers, and he lived mostly in extreme poverty. Schubert, who had a great melodic gift, is the acknowledged creator of the Romantic art song (lied), and he wrote over six hundred songs (lieder). He also wrote nine symphonies (including the famous *Unfinished Symphony*), religious works, choral music, operas, chamber music, and numerous piano solo and duet works.

Robert Schumann (1810–1856) was a German composer and pianist, who wrote his first piano pieces when he was seven. In 1832, Schumann injured his right hand and began to devote his energies to composition rather than playing the piano. In 1840, Schumann married Clara Wieck, a brilliant pianist who performed many of his works. Schumann wrote about other musicians in his magazine, *The New Music Journal*; he was the first to report on the importance of Chopin and Brahms. In 1850, Schumann was appointed Musical Director for the city of Düsseldorf. He held that position until 1853 when mental illness compelled him to resign. His compositions include symphonies, many piano works, a piano concerto, chamber music, songs, and choral works.

Fritz Spindler (1817–1905) was a German pianist, teacher, and composer. He lived in Dresden, where he had great success as a teacher. He wrote many sonatinas for his students.

Peter Ilyich Tchaikovsky (1840–1893), a Russian composer, studied with Anton Rubinstein at the Moscow Conservatory. Tchaikovsy became a professor of harmony at the Conservatory when he was twenty-six. He was supported through financial difficulties by Madame von Meck, a wealthy widow whom he never met. The security of the stipend he received from her enabled him to compose a great quantity of music. He traveled to America in 1891, where he was well received as a composer. His works include the ballets *Swan Lake*, *Sleeping Beauty*, and *The Nutcracker*; the *Piano Concerto in B-flat Minor*; many orchestral works, choral music, chamber music, songs, and piano music.